# SOCIAL & EMOTIONAL LEARNING CURRICULUM

By Mary Birdsell and Jo Meserve Mach
Photography by Mary Birdsell

### FINDING MY WAY

**The Finding My Way six-book series introduces kindergarten through 3rd grade children to both peers and adults with disabilities living inclusive lives.**

### SEL CURRICULUM

**The Finding My Way literature-based SEL curriculum promotes the development of skills needed for self-awareness. Lessons combine social and emotional learning with story time and activities based on components defined in the CASEL self-awareness competency.**

© 2021 Mary Birdsell, Jo Meserve Mach

These activities may be reproduced solely for classroom use and may not be used or posted online.

Finding My Way SEL Curriculum

Finding My Way Books
3512 SW Huntoon St.
Topeka, Kansas 66604
www.findingmywaybooks.com

(785) 273-6239

ISBN: 978-1-94754-135-1

Printed in the United States

10 9 8 7 6 5 4 3 2 1

For more information or to contact the author, please go to www.findingmywaybooks.com.

# SEL CURRICULUM                                            FINDING MY WAY SERIES

The **Finding My Way** book series presents diverse nonfiction stories that give voice to children with disabilities and promote their equity within our communities. Inclusive stories offer students the opportunity to meet children and adults with disabilities.

For each SEL lesson, we have linked a book to the self-awareness competency. Students gain context to develop competency capacities by reading the stories, learning background information, understanding different disability diagnoses, answering three styles of discussion questions, and completing activities.

## Social and Emotional Learning

**Self-awareness:** The abilities to understand one's own emotions, thoughts, and values and how they influence behavior across contexts. This includes capacities to recognize one's strengths and limitations with a well-grounded sense of confidence. Such as:

- *Integrating personal and social identities*
- *Identifying personal, cultural, and linguistic assets*
- *Demonstrating honesty and integrity*
- *Linking feelings, values, and thoughts*
- *Examining prejudices and biases*
- *Experiencing self-efficacy*
- *Having a growth mindset*
- *Developing interests and a sense of purpose*

www.casel.org/what-is-SEL

Begin and end curriculum with the **student survey** (page 42). Collecting this data offers you an opportunity to explore how the curriculum affected students' feelings about individuals with disabilities.

ABOUT THE CO-AUTHORS AND PHOTOGRAPHER

**Mary Birdsell** has authored nine children's books and is a former Speech and Theater teacher with an enthusiasm for all styles of learners. Mary believes everyone learns, creates, and has a story to tell. As a photographer, she strives to create images that reflect the strengths of each child. She uses colors and shapes to tell a story. For her, each book is like its own theater production.

**Jo Meserve Mach** is co-author of the Finding My Way Book Set. After working 36 years as an Occupational Therapist, she is very passionate about sharing the stories of children with special needs. Jo embraces the joy that individuals with disabilities bring to our communities through their unique gifts.

Finding My Way SEL Curriculum

## Table of Contents

*I Don't Know If I Want a Puppy* .................................................................................................. 1
    Family Feelings ........................................................................................................................ 3
    My Purpose .............................................................................................................................. 4
    Pantomime .............................................................................................................................. 5
    A Surprise Bookmark ............................................................................................................... 6

*I Want to Be Like Poppin' Joe* ...................................................................................................... 7
    What I Like to Do .................................................................................................................... 9
    Putting Things in Order ........................................................................................................ 10
    Taking the Hot Seat! ............................................................................................................. 11
    What Happens Next? ............................................................................................................ 12

*Kaitlyn Wants to See Ducks* ...................................................................................................... 13
    What Are My Feelings? ......................................................................................................... 15
    It's Hard to Wait .................................................................................................................... 16
    Reader's Theater Script and Discussion ............................................................................... 17

*Marco and I Want to Play Ball* .................................................................................................. 22
    Playing Fair ............................................................................................................................ 24
    The Real Me .......................................................................................................................... 25
    Pantomime ............................................................................................................................ 26
    Let's Start a Book Club ......................................................................................................... 27

*Waylen Wants to Jam* ............................................................................................................... 28
    Learning to Play the Drum ................................................................................................... 30
    Being Part of a Group .......................................................................................................... 31
    Reader's Theater Script and Discussion ............................................................................... 32

*OE Wants It to Be Friday* .......................................................................................................... 35
    How Would I Feel? ............................................................................................................... 37
    Talking Without Talking ....................................................................................................... 38
    Taking the Hot Seat! ............................................................................................................. 39
    An OE Book Report .............................................................................................................. 40

**Finding My Way SEL Activities Key** ........................................................................................ 41

**Finding My Way SEL Student Survey** ..................................................................................... 42

**Data Collection** ...................................................................................................................... 43

**Self-Awareness Award** ........................................................................................................... 44

# SEL CURRICULUM

# I DON'T KNOW IF I WANT A PUPPY

*Genre*: Nonfiction
*GRL*: E
*Interest level*: Pre-K-3
*Lexile*: 240

*SEL Self-awareness competency*: developing interests and a sense of purpose; linking feelings, values, and thoughts

*Disabilities represented*: congenital heart defect, speech/language delay

*Vocabulary*:
puppy
scared
outside
roll
messes
sad

The **Finding My Way** book series presents diverse nonfiction stories that give voice to children with disabilities and promote their equity within our communities. Inclusive stories offer students the opportunity to meet children and adults with disabilities.

## Summary

Ethan's older brothers want a puppy. Ethan likes to play with his cars and doesn't think it's a good idea to get a puppy. After a puppy arrives, the older brothers discover how much work a puppy requires. Ethan discovers he is much more qualified to take care of the puppy than his brothers.

## Background

Ethan was born with a heart defect. As a baby, he spent a lot of time in the hospital having heart surgeries and receiving special medical care.

His medical needs delayed his development. He didn't get to play and explore like most babies get to do. At school, Ethan

*Congenital heart defects are conditions that are present at birth and can affect the structure of a baby's heart and the way it works. They are the most common type of birth defect.* cdc.gov

needed extra support because others struggled to understand his speech.

We photographed his story when Ethan was in kindergarten and just beginning school.

Ethan has worked very hard over the years to speak more clearly. When he was in 5th grade, he read *I Don't Know If I Want a Puppy* out loud for an all-school talent night. He was very brave!

*"Ethan's story clearly illustrates how young children's self-determination can be nurtured when they are supported in making choices, provided opportunities to be capable, and understand how their actions affect others. All families, teachers, and caregivers can use this family's story to discuss and support the development of self-determination in their children."* Dr. Chelie Nelson, CCC-SLP

Self-awareness competency: developing interests and a sense of purpose; linking feelings, values, and thoughts

# SEL CURRICULUM

## I DON'T KNOW IF I WANT A PUPPY

### Pre-Reading Questions

1. Hold up the front cover. Why is this book nonfiction?
2. What do you think the story is about?
3. What is Ethan feeling on the cover?
4. Hold up the back cover. What do you think the colors mean?
5. Read the back of the book. What is it like to get a new pet?
6. What is a congenital heart defect?

### Discussion Questions

1. Why do Joe and Jake want a puppy?
2. How would you feel if you got a puppy?
3. How do you know if your mom is sad? What can you do to help?
4. What does it mean to take responsibility?
5. What are your responsibilities?
6. How does having responsibilities give you a purpose?

### Comprehension Questions

1. How do Joe and Jake feel in the book?
2. How does Ethan feel?
3. How does Emma feel?
4. Why does Mom get sad?
5. What do Ethan and Emma both like to do?
6. How can Ethan help Emma?

## Activities

### Family Feelings

Ethan talks about feelings in his book.
Sometimes he tells us how someone feels. Sometimes we can understand what someone feels by what they say. This activity reviews feelings in the book. Students identify the feelings.

### Finding My Purpose

Ethan liked to play with cars. He didn't know if he wanted his family to have a puppy. He wasn't sure about trying something new. After they got their puppy, Ethan learned some unexpected things about himself. As a result, he learned about his purpose. This activity reviews what Ethan likes to do with Emma and the purpose he discovered.

### Pantomime

This is a theater inspired activity requiring students to act out a scene without using words.

### A Surprise Bookmark

Students create a fun bookmark with a surprise in the middle to help someone feel happy.

Self-awareness competency: developing interests and a sense of purpose; linking feelings, values, and thoughts

I Don't Know If I Want a Puppy

## Family Feelings

Name_____  Date_____

Use a word or phrase from the box to fill in the blanks.
Your sentence will tell how each family member feels.

When Ethan is playing with cars and thinking about a

puppy, Ethan_____ how he feels.

> doesn't know
>
> happy
>
> sad
>
> scared

When Emma first comes to Ethan's home, Emma is _____.

When Mom knows that Joe and Jake don't want Emma, Mom is _____.

When Ethan plays with Emma, Ethan is _____.

How would you feel if you were Ethan? Circle the face that matches your feelings.

Self-awareness competency: developing interests and a sense of purpose; linking feelings, values, and thoughts

I Don't Know If I Want a Puppy

## Finding My Purpose

Name_____    Date_____

Color the bone if the sentence says what Ethan likes to do with Emma.

🦴 Ethan likes to give Emma hugs.

🦴 Ethan likes to give Emma kisses.

🦴 Ethan likes to jump with Emma.

🦴 Ethan likes to roller skate with Emma.

🦴 Ethan likes to go outside with Emma.

🦴 Ethan likes to roll around with Emma.

🦴 Ethan likes to go swimming with Emma.

🦴 Ethan likes to be with Emma.

Circle the answer.

Is Ethan's purpose to make his mom worry about Emma?    Yes    No

Is Ethan's purpose to take care of Emma so his mom doesn't worry?    Yes    No

Self-awareness competency: developing interests and a sense of purpose; linking feelings, values, and thoughts

I Don't Know If I Want a Puppy

## *Pantomime*

Students act out a scene without using words. Break students into small groups to act out parts of *I Don't Know If I Want a Puppy*. After each group has time to practice and prepare, have groups present their pantomimes in the order they happen in the book.

Roles do not have to be played by any specific gender. The goal is to communicate the action and feeling of a story without speaking.

Students can expand on the events depicted in the book. For example, Jake and Joe may try to get Dad to take Emma on a walk because they don't want to.

Group 1–Joe, Jake, Ethan, and Mom

    Joe and Jake beg for a dog. Ethan isn't sure. Mom decides.

Group 2–Joe, Jake, Mom, Dad, and Emma

    Mom and Dad bring Emma home. Jake and Joe have to learn to take care of her.

Group 3–Joe, Jake, Emma, Mom and Ethan

    Jake and Joe want to give Emma back. Mom gets sad. Ethan thinks about helping.

Group 4–Ethan, Emma, Mom

    Ethan takes care of Emma. Mom is proud of Ethan.

Self-awareness competency: developing interests and a sense of purpose; linking feelings, values, and thoughts

I Don't Know If I Want a Puppy

## A Surprise Bookmark

Name_____          Date_____

Cut out the big rectangle. Fold each side into the middle section. Now you have a long thin rectangle with a hidden part. Decorate your bookmark. Draw or write something fun in the middle as a surprise for someone you want to feel happy.

Self-awareness competency: developing interests and a sense of purpose; linking feelings, values, and thoughts

# SEL CURRICULUM                    I WANT TO BE LIKE POPPIN' JOE

*Genre*: Nonfiction
*GRL*: H
*Interest level*: Pre-K-3
*Lexile*: 270

*SEL Self-awareness competency*: identifying personal, cultural, and linguistic assets; having a growth mindset

*Disabilities represented*: Down syndrome, autism

*Vocabulary*:
popcorn
juggle
weigh
dump
rake
boss

The **Finding My Way** book series presents diverse nonfiction stories that give voice to children with disabilities and promote their equity within our communities. Inclusive stories offer students the opportunity to meet children and adults with disabilities.

## Summary
Dylan is a young boy with Down syndrome. He compares how he helps his dad do yard work with what Poppin' Joe does as he works with his dad. He learns how Joe followed his interests to find a job he likes. Dylan realizes he can be like Joe, who has Down syndrome and autism.

## Background
Joe grew up in a small-town where staff did not allow him to be in the public swimming pool as a young boy because he had a disability. His teachers said Joe would never get a job because he had a poor attention span.

> **Down syndrome** is a condition in which a person has an extra chromosome. Even though people with Down syndrome might act and look similar, each person has different abilities. People with Down syndrome usually have an IQ in the mildly-to-moderately low range and are slower to speak than other children. cdc.gov

Joe says only a few words. His parents taught him how to be social, using greetings and smiles. When he was young, they gave him the same opportunities that they gave his older siblings. Visit Poppin' Joe's website to learn about Joe's success.

We photographed this story when Dylan was six years old. A few years later, Dylan started his own business selling dog treats.

> People with **autism** often have problems with social, emotional, and communication skills. They might repeat certain behaviors and might not want change in their daily activities. Many people with autism also have different ways of learning, paying attention, or reacting to things. cdc.gov

> "Dylan's classmates have a better understanding and more patience when interacting with him daily. Learning opportunities have grown with Dylan and the whole class because of this new found understanding brought on by this book." Mandy Yoder, Dylan's 1st grade teacher

Self-awareness competency: identifying personal, cultural, and linguistic assets, having a growth mindset

# SEL CURRICULUM — I WANT TO BE LIKE POPPIN' JOE

### Pre-Reading Questions

1. Hold up the front cover. Why is this book nonfiction?
2. What do you think the story is about?
3. What are Poppin' Joe and Dylan doing on the cover?
4. Hold up the back cover. What do you think the colors mean?
5. Read the back of the book. What kind of job would you like?
6. What is Down syndrome?
7. What is autism?

### Discussion Questions

1. Why is Poppin' Joe a good friend for Dylan?
2. What are your interests?
3. How can your interests help you pick a job?
4. If something is hard, should you stop trying?
5. What do you learn if you don't succeed the first time?
6. How could you be like Poppin' Joe?

### Comprehension Questions

1. What does Poppin' Joe like to do?
2. What does he like best?
3. What does Dylan like to do?
4. How did Poppin' Joe pick his job?
5. What are the steps in Poppin' Joe's job?
6. What could Dylan's job be when he grows up?

## Activities

### *What I Like to Do*

Joe and Dylan share what they like to do. By following his interests, Joe found a job he liked. This activity encourages students to consider their interests and what kind of job they might want to do.

### *Putting Things in Order*

Joe's job has many parts. Dylan talks about each part and how he can do it, too. How does Dylan feel about completing all those parts? This activity helps students gain an understanding that there are important parts to every job.

### *Taking the HOT SEAT!*

One student at a time sits in the `hot seat' and answers questions as if they were a character from the book, *I Want to Be Like Poppin' Joe*.

### *What Happens Next?*

This activity gives students the opportunity to imagine what might happen next in this story.

Self-awareness competency: identifying personal, cultural, and linguistic assets, having a growth mindset

I Want to Be Like Poppin' Joe

## *What I Like to Do*

Name_____     Date_____

Dylan likes to be outside.     Dylan likes to play with his dog.

Draw two pictures of what you like to do. Finish the sentences below.

I like to _____. I like to_____.

This is a job I'd like to do: _____.

Self-awareness competency: identifying personal, cultural, and linguistic assets, having a growth mindset

I Want to Be Like Poppin' Joe

## *Putting Things in Order*

Name_____     Date_____

Poppin' Joe's job has many parts. Put the parts in order with numbers 1-6.

_____ listens to corn popping

_____ loads popcorn

_____ mixes corn, sugar, and oil

_____ dumps popcorn

_____ shovels popcorn

_____ salts popcorn

You want to play ball. Put in order what you need to do with numbers 1-6.

_____ get your ball

_____ tell your friends you want to play ball

_____ put on your play clothes

_____ ask Mom or Dad if you can go

_____ do your homework

_____ decide what game to play

Self-awareness competency: identifying personal, cultural, and linguistic assets, having a growth mindset

I Want to Be Like Poppin' Joe

## *Taking the HOT SEAT!*

One student at a time sits in the 'hot seat' and answers questions, as if they were a character from the book, *I Want to Be Like Poppin' Joe*. Roles do not have to be played by any specific gender.

Below are examples of questions and answers. If the book hasn't given an answer to a question that is asked, the person in the 'hot seat' gets to decide what they think the answer would be.

**Questions for Poppin' Joe**

What do you like to do? *(clean cars, fill cups, hang out with Dad, juggle, make popcorn, stay busy)*

What is your job? *(making popcorn)*

What is your favorite food? *(popcorn)*

Where do you sell popcorn? *(fairs, farmers' market, stores)*

How did you get your nickname? *(Joe became Poppin' Joe when he became known for his popcorn)*

**Questions for Dylan**

What do you like to do? *(play with his dog, give hugs, hang out with Dad, dig, be outside)*

What do you do to help your dad? *(mix fertilizer, weigh plants, count plants, dump dirt, rake, shovel, load)*

Who else helps your dad? *(brother, dog)*

What is your favorite color? *(blue because he's wearing a blue shirt)*

What do you want to be when you grow up? *(the boss)*

Self-awareness competency: identifying personal, cultural, and linguistic assets, having a growth mindset

I Want to Be Like Poppin' Joe

# What Happens Next?

Name_____     Date_____

1. Write a sentence about what happens next in *I Want to Be Like Poppin' Joe*.

    You can write about what Dylan does next.

    Or you can write about what Joe does next.

    Or you can write about what they do next together.

    _____

    _____

2. Draw a picture about what happens next. It should go with your sentence.

Self-awareness competency: identifying personal, cultural, and linguistic assets, having a growth mindset

# SEL CURRICULUM                                    KAITLYN WANTS TO SEE DUCKS

*Genre*: Nonfiction
*GRL*: F
*Interest level*: Pre-K-3
*Lexile*: 280

*SEL Self-awareness competency*: identifying one's emotions, experiencing self-efficacy

*Disability represented*: Down syndrome

*Vocabulary*:
zoo
swim
roar
silly
dirty
hungry
whisper

The **Finding My Way** book series presents diverse nonfiction stories that give voice to children with disabilities and promote their equity within our communities. Inclusive stories offer students the opportunity to meet children and adults with disabilities.

## Summary
It's family day at the zoo. Kaitlyn only wants to see the ducks. While her family stops to see all the different animals, she struggles with waiting. When they finally arrive at the duck pond, there are no ducks! Her family helps her find them.

## Background
Kaitlyn has Down syndrome and is the oldest child in her family. We photographed her story when she was in 1st grade. She has younger twin sisters.

Going to the zoo is very important to Kaitlyn's parents. Her family goes frequently and takes the same route through the zoo. This gives all three girls a chance to see many animals.

> ***Down syndrome*** *is a condition in which a person has an extra chromosome…*
> *… Even though people with Down syndrome might act or look similar, each person has different abilities. People with Down syndrome usually have an IQ in the mild-to moderately low range and are slower to speak than other children.*
> cdc.gov

They like to go early in the morning when there are fewer people at the zoo.

Kaitlyn loves water, so she enjoys anything that has water at the zoo. Seeing the hippos, fish, and alligators in the water is fun. Visiting the zoo after it rains is extra fun because there are puddles to play in. Kaitlyn also likes waterfalls, drinking fountains, and hoses spraying water.

> *"Kaitlyn Wants to See Ducks realistically portrays the challenges and rewards that come daily to Kaitlyn's family. I feel this book will help all students learn that sometimes resisting temptation for an immediate reward, leads to gratification in the end."* Katherine Cooney, Ed.M. Kaitlyn's Elementary School Principal

Self-awareness competency: identifying one's emotions, experiencing self-efficacy

# SEL CURRICULUM

## KAITLYN WANTS TO SEE DUCKS

### Pre-Reading Questions

1. Hold up the front cover. Why is this book nonfiction?
2. What do you think the story is about?
3. What does Kaitlyn feel on the cover?
4. Hold up the back cover. What do you think the colors mean?
5. Read the back of the book. What do you like to do at the zoo?
6. What is Down syndrome?

### Discussion Questions

1. Who do you like to go to the zoo with?
2. What animals do you like to see?
3. Does your family like to see the same animals?
4. How do you feel at the zoo?
5. Do you like to wait?
6. What do you do while you're waiting?

### Comprehension Questions

1. What is Kaitlyn's favorite animal at the zoo?
2. What do the apes do?
3. Who lives next door to the apes?
4. What do the elephants do?
5. Which animals do Paige and Alexis feed?
6. What do the ducks do?
7. How does each family member feel at the zoo?

## Activities

### What Are My Feelings?

Kaitlyn struggles through many emotions as she waits to see the ducks. What is she feeling while she waits? What do you feel when you have to wait for something you really want? This activity asks students to identify Kaitlyn's feelings and then identify their own feelings.

### It's Hard to Wait

Kaitlyn waits a long time to see the ducks. What does she do that helps her wait? What can you do to help you wait? This activity gives students the opportunity to consider activities to help them through times when they have to wait for something.

### Reader's Theater Script and Discussion

This activity gives students the opportunity to act out Kaitlyn's story. To encourage audience interpretation, facilitate a discussion using the list of questions.

Self-awareness competency: identifying one's emotions, experiencing self-efficacy

Kaitlyn Wants to See Ducks

## *What Are My Feelings?*

Name_____     Date_____

Circle the animal Kaitlyn wants to see.

How many different animals did Kaitlyn see? _____

Circle how Kaitlyn feels when she is waiting to see ducks.

Circle how you feel when you have to wait.

Circle how Kaitlyn feels when she sees the ducks.

Circle how you feel when you get what you're waiting for.

Self-Awareness competency: identifying one's emotions, experiencing self-efficacy

Kaitlyn Wants to See Ducks

## *It's Hard to Wait*

Name_____  Date_____

Kaitlyn had to wait to see the ducks. <u>Draw a line under</u> what she did while she was waiting.

ate a snack

watched water falling

looked at other animals

sang a song

had a ride on Dad's back

jumped up and down

Draw a picture of what you do when you're waiting.

Self-awareness competency: identifying one's emotions, experiencing self-efficacy

## *Kaitlyn Wants to See Ducks:* Reader's Theater Script

**Roles**: Narrator, Kaitlyn, Mom, Dad, Alexis, Paige, apes (mom and baby), lions (1 or 2), giraffes (2), goats (mom and baby), bears (2), ducks (5-10)

**Props**: toys for apes to play with, pretend dirt, pretend green leaves to feed giraffes

**Setting**: zoo

NARRATOR: It's family day at the zoo.

> This is Kaitlyn.
>
> She loves to swim.
>
> Ducks love to swim, too.
>
> Kaitlyn thinks ducks are the best animals.

KAITLYN: Let's see ducks!

MOM: I think there are a lot of fun animals.

> Let's go see the apes.

KAITLYN: Let's see ducks.

DAD: Kaitlyn, are the apes outside or inside?

NARRATOR: They are inside. (*Mom and baby ape play.*)

ALEXIS and PAIGE: We like the baby ape.

NARRATOR: Kaitlyn likes the water falling.

> It's loud and wet.
>
> Those apes are silly.
>
> Those silly apes don't swim.

KAITLYN: Let's see ducks.

MOM: (Mom *roars like a lion and does sign language for lion.*)

> Who lives next door?

ALEXIS and PAIGE: (*Alexis and Paige do sign language for lion.*)

> The lions, the lions!

Kaitlyn Wants to See Ducks

DAD: Stand close. (*The lions are sleeping*)

    Can you hear the lions?

NARRATOR: No, the lions are sleeping.

    Those sleepy lions don't swim.

KAITLYN: Let's see ducks. (*Kaitlyn is lying on the ground.*)

MOM: Who can sign elephant? (*Mom signs elephant.*)

NARRATOR: Will the elephants get a bath? (*The elephants play in the dirt.*)

    No, not today.

    They play in the dirt.

    Those dirty elephants don't swim.

KAITLYN: Let's see ducks! (*Kaitlyn is yelling.*)

MOM: Who wants to feed the giraffes?

ALEXIS and PAIGE: We want to feed the giraffes. (*They feed giraffes some leaves.*)

NARRATOR: Those hungry giraffes don't swim.

KAITLYN: Let's see ducks.

DAD: The goats and bears are next.

NARRATOR: Kaitlyn looks at her family.

    Mom likes to talk to animals. (*Mom talks to the goats.*)

    Alexis and Paige like to feed animals and find baby animals. (*They feed goats.*)

    Dad likes to see all the animals. (*Dad watches the bears play.*)

KAITLYN: Let's see ducks. (*Kaitlyn feels upset and holds her head.*)

DAD: It's time to see ducks!

Kaitlyn Wants to See Ducks

NARRATOR: Oh no, where are the ducks? (*The ducks are hiding.*)

    Dad looks for ducks.

    Mom looks for ducks.

    Alexis looks for ducks.

    Paige looks for ducks.

    Kaitlyn looks for ducks.

NARRATOR: Kaitlyn's family wants to help her find the ducks.
(*The ducks come out of their hiding places.*)

    Kaitlyn sees something silly.     (*One duck has its bottom in the air.*)

    Kaitlyn sees ducks sleeping.

    Kaitlyn sees dirty ducks.

    Kaitlyn sees hungry ducks.

    Kaitlyn sees ducks swimming.

    Kaitlyn is happy.

    She found her ducks.

## Reader's Theater: Discussion Questions for Audience Interpretation

1. How does Kaitlyn feel at the beginning of the play?
2. How does Kaitlyn feel in the middle of the play?
3. How does Kaitlyn feel at the end of the play?
4. What kind of movements make people look like animals?
5. How can you tell the difference between the animals the actors are pretending to be?
6. What do the ducks have in common with the other animals?
7. Kaitlyn's family all like different animals at the zoo. Is that the same for your family?
8. Is it fun for families to like different animals?
9. What does your family like to do?

Self-awareness competency: identifying one's emotions, experiencing self-efficacy

# SEL CURRICULUM                           MARCO AND I WANT TO PLAY BALL

*Genre*: Nonfiction
*GRL*: G
*Interest level*: Pre-K-3
*Lexile*: 350

*SEL Self-awareness competency*: integrating personal and social identities, demonstrating honesty and integrity

*Disability represented*: Spina bifida

*Vocabulary*:
snore
misses
slam
fly ball
batter up
barn

The **Finding My Way** book series presents diverse nonfiction stories that give voice to children with disabilities and promote their equity within our communities. Inclusive stories offer students the opportunity to meet children and adults with disabilities.

## Summary

Isiah and Marco are cousins who both love to play baseball. They are visiting their grandpa and want to go outside and play with him. All three have fun, as the cousins compete to see who can hit the barn when it's their turn at bat.

## Background

We photographed this story when Isiah started 2nd grade, and Marco started kindergarten. They are both growing up biracial. Marco is Hispanic/White. Isiah is Black/White. They are very best friends and cousins.

Isiah was born with Spina bifida. He didn't learn to walk independently until he was three years old. He wears leg braces and cannot run. This does not stop him from loving any kind of ball game.

*Spina bifida is a birth defect that occurs when the spine and spinal cord don't form properly... It's a type of neural tube defect. In babies with Spina bifida, a portion of the neural tube doesn't close or develop properly, causing defects in the spinal cord and in the bones of the spine... Spina bifida can range from mild to severe, depending on the type of defect, size, location and complications.* mayoclinic.org

Marco is very accepting of Isiah's physical limitations. It doesn't matter to him that Isiah needs some assistance when they play together. You can see in his book that their grandpa set up a slide in the middle of the backfield of their baseball game so Isiah can slide in from outfield. This saves him time from having to walk so far when they play.

*"Isiah's perseverance to participate and determination to succeed, makes a physical therapist's job easy and has been an inspiration to me and many others. This book aptly captures the drive that fuels Isiah and his family."* Muriel Hinshaw, PT, Isiah's school physical therapist

Self-awareness competency: integrating personal and social identities, demonstrating honesty and integrity

# SEL CURRICULUM

**MARCO AND I WANT TO PLAY BALL**

### Pre-Reading Questions

1. Hold up the front cover. Why is this book nonfiction?
2. What do you think the story is about?
3. What are Marco and Isiah doing on the cover?
4. Hold up the back cover. What do you think the colors mean?
5. Read the back of the book. What do you like to do with your cousins?
6. What is Spina bifida?

### Discussion Questions

1. Why are sports and games fun?
2. Could you still play sports if you couldn't run?
3. Why do games have rules?
4. Is it important to follow the rules?
5. Do you ever tease your cousins or siblings? Is that okay?
6. What do you think when you see someone wearing leg braces?

### Comprehension Questions

1. What do Isiah and Marco like to play?
2. Who do they like to play with?
3. Who bats first?
4. How does Isiah come in to bat?
5. Where do they lose a ball?
6. What are Marco and Isiah trying to hit with the ball?

## Activities

### *Playing Fair*

Isiah and Marco love to play together. They tease each other with their words, but they always play fair with each other. They respect each other and care about each other's feelings. This activity encourages students to consider the way Isiah and Marco play together.

### *The Real Me*

We don't realize how quickly we decide about others just by looking at them. Isiah has a physical disability, and many people judge him on that alone. This activity inspires students to be more open in their thoughts of others.

### *Pantomime*

This is a theater inspired activity requiring students to act out a scene without using words.

### *Let's Start a Book Club*

This activity provides questions for a thoughtful book club gathering.

Self-awareness competency: integrating personal and social identities, demonstrating honesty and integrity

Marco and I Want to Play Ball

## *Playing Fair*

Name_____     Date_____

When you play fair, you treat everyone the same way. <u>Draw a line under</u> the answer that shows Isiah and Marco playing fair.

When it's time to pick up the balls, Marco has to pick them up.

When it's time to pick up the balls, Marco and Isiah pick them up.

When the ball gets stuck in a tree, Isiah and Marco get it out together.

When the ball gets stuck in the tree, Isiah has to get it by himself.

Only Marco gets to bat the ball.

Marco and Isiah take turns batting the ball.

Isiah pretends he catches the ball when he didn't catch it.

Isiah and Marco show each other when they catch or drop a ball.

Self-awareness competency: integrating personal and social identities, demonstrating honesty and integrity

Marco and I Want to Play Ball

## The Real Me

Name_____   Date_____

How do you think of Isiah? Circle your answer.

a boy who wears leg braces

a boy who loves baseball

a boy who has fun with his cousin

a boy who can't run

How do you want others to think of you?

_____

_____

Why?

_____

_____

Self-awareness competency: integrating personal and social identities, demonstrating honesty and integrity

Marco and I Want to Play Ball

## *Pantomime*

Students act out a scene without using words. Break students into small groups to act out parts of *Marco and I Want to Play Ball*. After each group has time to practice and prepare, have groups present their pantomimes in the order they happen in the book.

Roles do not have to be played by any specific gender. The goal is to communicate the action and feeling of a story without speaking.

Students can expand on the events depicted in the book. For example, Marco may run some bases, or small groups could act out other parts of a baseball game with more players.

Group 1-Grandpa, Isiah, Marco

    Isiah and Marco want to play ball. Grandpa takes a nap first.

Group 2-Grandpa, Isiah, Marco

    Marco bats first. Isiah catches a ball Marco hit. All the balls have to be picked up. Grandpa pitches.

Group 3-Grandpa, Isiah, Marco

    Isiah bats. One ball goes over Marco's head. Marco slides to catch it. Grandpa pitches.

Group 4-Grandpa, Isiah, Marco

    Marco is the batter. Isiah is the catcher. Marco gets a ball stuck in a tree. Isiah and Marco get the ball out without Grandpa's help. Grandpa pitches and then watches Isiah and Marco.

Group 5-Grandpa, Isiah, Marco

    Isiah bats. Marco is the catcher. Isiah keeps batting and Marco moves to the outfield. Isiah hits the barn with a ball. Grandpa pitches.

Self-awareness competency: integrating personal and social identities, demonstrating honesty and integrity

Marco and I Want to Play Ball

## Let's Start a Book Club

Name_____     Date_____

To start your book club, have everyone read Marco and I Want to Play Ball. Then get together. Answer these questions as you talk about the book.

What was the book about? _____

_____

_____

What did you like about the book? _____

_____

_____

What do you think happens next? _____

_____

Which person in the story would you like to know more about? _____

What would you like to know? _____

Would you recommend this book to a friend? _____ Why or why not? _____

_____

Self-awareness competency: integrating personal and social identities, demonstrating honesty and integrity

# SEL CURRICULUM                                              WAYLEN WANTS TO JAM

*Genre*: Nonfiction
*GRL*: J
*Interest level*: Pre-K-3
*Lexile*: 390

*SEL Self-awareness competency*:
developing interests and a sense of purpose, identifying personal and social identities

*Disability represented*: autism

*Vocabulary*:
hold in
snare drum
bass drum
jamming
silly pose
drumline moves

The **Finding My Way** book series presents diverse nonfiction stories that give voice to children with disabilities and promote their equity within our communities. Inclusive stories offer students the opportunity to meet children and adults with disabilities.

## Summary

Waylen is learning how to play on a drumline. His story shares his lessons and how he practices during his weekly class. His concert at the end of the book highlights how much he has learned as a member of a drumline.

## Background

Waylen is autistic. He has always liked to bang on things to make sounds. He loves music of all types.

Waylen listens to a song one time, and he can play its beat.

Waylen was in 2nd grade at the time we photographed his story. His 11-year-old brother had been on the drumline for several years, and Waylen really wanted to be a

> *People with **autism** often have problems with social, emotional, and communication skills. They might repeat certain behaviors and might not want change in their daily activities. Many people with autism also have different ways of learning, paying attention, or reacting to things. cdc.gov*

drummer like his brother. He was the first child with autism to be invited to join the community drumline program.

When you ask Waylen how he plays the drums, he answers by saying 1-2-3-4-5-6-7-8. Counting the beat is how he thinks of drumming.

> *"My 1st grade students remained engaged with this book from beginning to end! I opened our nonfiction unit with this book. Students learned vocabulary such as drumline and inclusion. I would highly recommend this book."* Marie, 1st grade teacher

Waylen's teacher, Sal, is a first generation Mexican American. When we finished the book, he spoke about how important the message of his inclusion and Waylen's inclusion were for his community and himself.

> *"Waylen's strength is his natural heart for music and the beat. When he plays, he smiles. He has a natural feel for it. He feels part of the team."* Sal Cruz, Waylen's drumline teacher

Self-awareness competency: developing interests and a sense of purpose, integrating personal and social identities

# SEL CURRICULUM — WAYLEN WANTS TO JAM

### Pre-Reading Questions

1. Hold up the front cover. Why is this book nonfiction?
2. What do you think the story is about?
3. What is Waylen doing on the cover?
4. Hold up the back cover. What do you think the colors and shapes mean?
5. Read the back of the book. Would you like to play the drums?
6. What is autism?

### Discussion Questions

1. Would you like to learn to play the drums?
2. What would it be like to be on a drumline?
3. Do you like being part of a team?
4. How does being on a team help you be the best you?
5. What kind of a group would you want to be a part of?
6. How are groups good for the community?

### Comprehension Questions

1. Who is Waylen's teacher?
2. What shape does Sal want the drumline to make with their sticks?
3. How is the song, *Hit the Drum,* played?
4. What happens if a drumline doesn't play together?
5. What are the drummers practicing for?
6. How does Waylen know he belongs on the drumline?

## Activities

### *Learning to Play the Drum*

Sal teaches Waylen and all the children how to play, step-by-step. They are learning how to become drummers on a drumline. This activity reminds students of the fun way Sal teaches drumming.

### *Being Part of a Group*

At the end of Waylen's story, he shares he knows this is where he belongs. We all have those places, activities, or groups where we feel the same way. This activity gives students the opportunity to design a t-shirt for a group where they feel they would belong.

### *Reader's Theater Script and Discussion*

This activity gives students the opportunity to act out Waylen's story. To encourage audience interpretation, facilitate a discussion using the list of questions.

Self-awareness competency: developing interests and a sense of purpose, integrating personal and social identities

Waylen Wants to Jam

## *Learning to Play the Drum*

Name_____  Date_____

Use a word or phrase from the box to fill in the blanks.

| |
|---|
| drumline |
| hold in |
| listen |
| pizza |
| silly |
| song |
| trick |

Sal tells us to _____ our sticks.

Sal tells us to place our sticks like a slice of _____.

Sal shows us a stick _____.

Sal teaches us how to play a_____.

Sal shows us a_____ pose.

Sal tells us we need to _____ when playing on a _____.

Self-awareness competency: developing interests and a sense of purpose, integrating personal and social identities

Waylen Wants to Jam

## *Being Part of a Group*

Name_____     Date_____

Design a t-shirt for a group where you belong.

What kind of group is it? _____

Self-awareness competency: developing interests and a sense of purpose, integrating personal and social identities

*Waylen Wants to Jam:* Reader's Theater Script

**Roles**: Narrator, Waylen, Sal, students in drumline class

**Props**: drum sticks and drums, larger drum, matching colored t-shirts for concert scene

**Setting**: drum classroom, concert


NARRATOR: Waylen loves to play the drums.

    He's learning to play on a drumline.

    How do you play the drums, Waylen?

WAYLEN: 1-2-3-4-5-6-7-8 (*Waylen hits the drum as he shouts out each number.*)

NARRATOR: Waylen is showing us how he counts every time he hits the drum.

    (*Sal and all the drummers walk to the front. They have drumsticks and a drum.*)

NARRATOR: This is Waylen's drum class.

    Sal is their teacher.

    He tells them what to do.

    He shows them what to do.

SAL: Hold in your sticks.

NARRATOR: Sal shows them how to hold their sticks together *(All the drummers hold in their sticks.)*

WAYLEN: I can hold in my sticks.

SAL: This is how you hold your sticks to play. *(All the drummers hold their sticks to play.)*

NARRATOR: Sal is showing them how to hold their sticks in the fold of their fingers.

WAYLEN: I can hold my sticks like Sal.

SAL: This is how you place your sticks. *(All the drummers make a piece of pizza with their sticks.)*

NARRATOR: Sal is showing them how to place their sticks so they look like a slice of pizza.

WAYLEN: I can place my sticks like Sal.

SAL: I am going to show you how to do a stick trick.

NARRATOR: Sal throws his stick up and catches it. *(All the drummers try to do the stick trick.)*

Waylen Wants to Jam

WAYLEN: Whoops! My stick flew out of hand.

    Whew! I'm glad it didn't hit anyone.

SAL: It's time to learn a song.

NARRATOR: Everyone needs to hold in their sticks and watch Sal.

    It's hard to wait and not play.

SAL: The song is 'Hit-the-drum.'

    The beat matches the words.

NARRATOR: Sal hits the drum with his right hand.

    He hits the drum with his left hand

    He hits the drum with his right hand again.

ALL: Hit-the-drum. *(Drummers play with Sal and say "Hit-the-drum" as they play the beat.)*

WAYLEN: Oops! I hit the drum next to me.

    It's hard to stop.

    I love to play the drums!

NARRATOR: Sal is jamming. *(Sal jams.)*

    He plays a fun beat.

    He wants all the students to copy his beat. *(All the drummers try to copy Sal's beat.)*

WAYLEN: Sometimes I close my eyes. *(Waylen closes his eyes as he tries to copy Sal's beat.)*

    That makes it easier to hear Sal.

    This is so fun.

    I can't stop playing!

    *(All the drummers are playing their own beat.)*

SAL: Stop! If you don't play together, you just make noise.

    We want to make music.

    Hold in your sticks.

    You need to listen. *(Sal jams.)*

NARRATOR: Everyone is listening. *(All the drummers play like Sal.)*

NARRATOR: They're learning to play like Sal.

> On a drumline everyone must play the same way.

SAL: Now I want everyone to take turns playing the bass drum.
*(Drummers line up by a large drum and take turns.)*

WAYLEN: *(Waylen sits on the floor and uses his sticks to keep the beat.)*

> It's hard to wait in line.

> I like to sit.

> I like to do something while I wait. *(Waylen practices his stick trick.)*

NARRATOR: Waylen gets his turn.

SAL: Now it's time to learn a drumline move. *(Sal shows them a drumline move.)*

NARRATOR: Sal steps and hits the drum.

> He yells, "I-I-I."

> He makes a silly pose.

> *(All drummers try to do the drumline move with Sal.)*

WAYLEN: I can be silly like Sal.

NARRATOR: They have to keep practicing, so they can do the moves together.

> They're getting ready for their spring concert.

> *(All drummers are getting better at doing the drumline move with Sal.)*

NARRATOR: It looks like they're ready.

> Let's watch their concert.

> *(Drummers all wear the same color shirt. They get in their drumline.)*

> *(Drummers play 'Hit-the-drum, do the silly pose move, and bow on the last beat.)*

WAYLEN: This is our drumline.

> I love playing the drums.

> I know this is where I belong.

Waylen Wants to Jam

## *Reader's Theater*: Discussion Questions for Audience Interpretation

1. How does Waylen play the drums?

2. How does Sal teach kids to be drummers?

3. What does Sal teach in the drum class?

4. Why do the drummers do the same thing at the same time?

5. How does doing the same thing together make a team?

6. What is it like to be a part of a team?

7. What do you like to do with a team?

8. Who leads the different teams you are on? (*teacher leads a class, coach leads a soccer team*)

9. What do you like about your leaders?

Self-awareness competency: developing interests and a sense of purpose, integrating personal and social identities

# SEL CURRICULUM                                OE WANTS IT TO BE FRIDAY

*Genre*: Nonfiction
*GRL*: K
*Interest level*: Pre-K-3
*Lexile*: 390

*SEL Self-awareness competency*: examining prejudices and biases; identifying personal, cultural, and linguistic assets

*Disability represented*: cerebral palsy (use of wheelchair and several communication devices)

*Vocabulary*:
sick
dance
spelling
gym
ramp
boccia

The **Finding My Way** book series presents diverse nonfiction stories that give voice to children with disabilities and promote their equity within our communities. Inclusive stories offer students the opportunity to meet children and adults with disabilities.

## Summary
OE's favorite activity happens on Friday. Each day of the week she shares what she is doing as she waits to go with her dad to play boccia on Friday.

## Background
OE and her coach Austin both have cerebral palsy and use communication devices or sign language to communicate. They are both inspirational in their personal motivation to be fully active within their home and communities.

An American family adopted OE from Russia when she was five years old. She spent the first years of her life lying in a crib. Her new parents wanted her to take part as fully as possible in her daily activities. She is very smart, but she has minimal muscle control and cannot speak. We photographed her story when OE was in 1st grade.

*Cerebral palsy (CP) is a group of disorders that affect a person's ability to move and maintain balance and posture. CP is the most common motor disability in childhood. Cerebral means having to do with the brain. Palsy means weakness or problems with using the muscles.*  cdc.gov

The first time OE went to boccia practice, she got extremely excited because there were other people in wheelchairs, just like her!

Austin Hanson started playing boccia when he was 12 years old. His step-father is his coach and ramp assistant. Since 1996, he has competed all over the world as a member of the US Paralympic Boccia Team. In 2016, Austin ranked as the #1 USA player and the #12 international player.

*"This book really captures the spirit of OE. She has the determination to do as much as she can! With such a wonderful spirit, she is loved by all who know her and is sought out by acquaintances when out and about. The book tells her story and how she loves to maximize her abilities. She is very smart, and it shows! The book will encourage others to 'be all they can be' and help those with lesser abilities to do the same. I love the book!"* Patty, friend of OE's family

Self-Awareness competency: examining prejudices and biases; identifying personal, cultural, and linguistic assets

# SEL CURRICULUM     OE WANTS IT TO BE FRIDAY

### Pre-Reading Questions

1. Hold up the front cover. Why is this book nonfiction?
2. What do you think the story is about?
3. What is OE doing on the cover?
4. Hold up the back cover. What do you think the colors and shapes mean?
5. Read the back of the book. What do you think Austin coaches?
6. What is cerebral palsy?

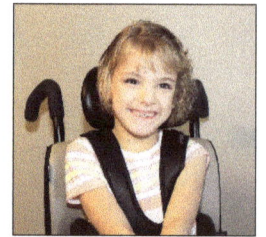

### Discussion Questions

1. What day of the week do you like best?
2. How do you feel about people who use a wheelchair?
3. What would it be like to use a wheelchair?
4. Austin has won gold medals in the Paralympics. What Paralympic sport would you want to play?
5. OE uses different communication boards. What would you put on your communication board?
6. How can you communicate in different ways?

### Comprehension Questions

1. What does OE stand for?
2. What does OE like to do in the car?
3. How does OE feel about boccia?
4. What is the white ball called?
5. How do you win boccia?
6. How does OE tell her dad to move the ramp?

## Activities

### How Would It Feel?

OE and Austin spend most of their day in a wheelchair because they cannot sit up by themselves. A wheelchair is a special chair. This activity gives students the opportunity to think about making a wheelchair as wonderful as possible.

### Talking Without Talking

OE and Austin can't use their voices to speak. They use communication devices or talking boards. This activity has students using alternative ways of communicating.

### Taking the HOT SEAT!

One student at a time sits in the 'hot seat' and answers questions as if they were a character from the book, *OE Wants It to Be Friday*.

### An OE Book Report

Students write a book report about OE's books and their feelings about her story.

Self-Awareness competency: examining prejudices and biases; identifying personal, cultural, and linguistic assets

OE Wants It to Be Friday

## *How Would It Feel?*

Name_____     Date_____

How would it feel to sit in a wheelchair? How different would it be from sitting in a regular chair? Draw yourself and decorate your wheelchair. Add color, cushions, cup holders, and anything fun you can imagine to your wheelchair.

Self-awareness competency: examining prejudices and biases, identifying personal, cultural, and linguistic assets

OE Wants It to Be Friday

## Talking Without Talking

Name_____     Date_____

Make a Talking Board. Color the first circle red and the second circle green.

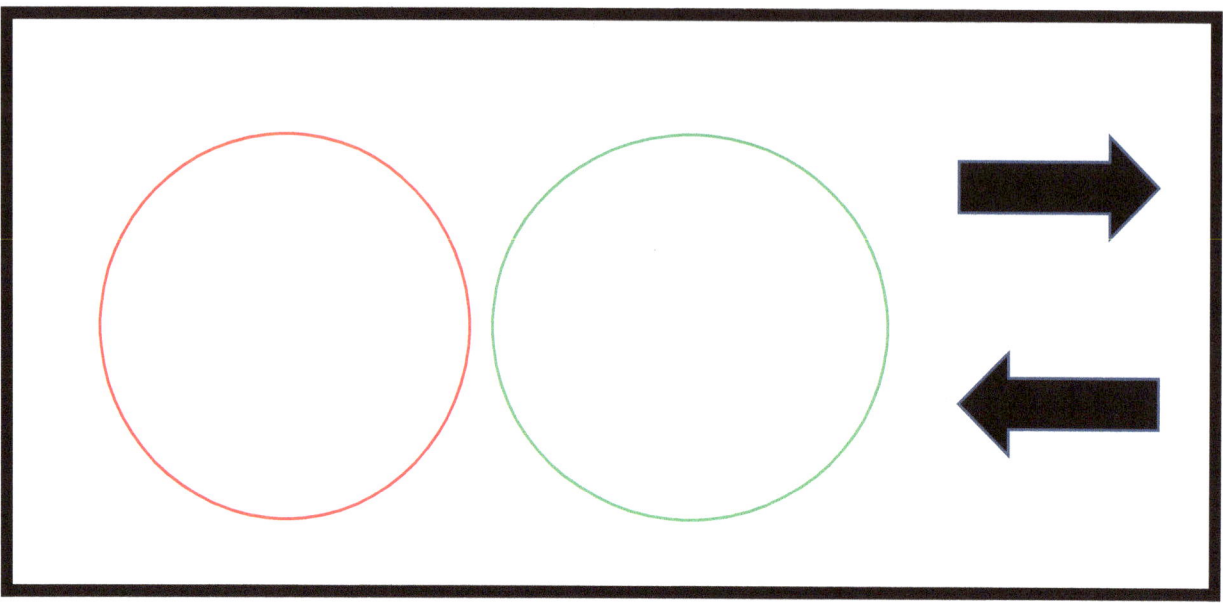

Get a buddy.

Go for a walk together.

Do not use your voice to talk. Use your talking board.

Point to the green circle to walk. Point to the red circle to stop.

Point to the arrows to turn to the left or the right.

When done, tell your buddy 'thank you' in sign language.

> To **sign thank you**, make your hand flat. Touch your fingers to your chin and then move your hand forward. Smile.

Self-awareness competency: examining prejudices and biases, identifying personal, cultural, and linguistic assets

OE Wants It to Be Friday

## *Taking the HOT SEAT!*

One student at a time sits in the 'hot seat' and answers questions as if they were a character from the book, *OE Wants It to Be Friday*. Roles do not have to be played by any specific gender.

Below are examples of questions and answers. If the book hasn't given an answer to a question that is asked, the person in the 'hot seat' gets to decide what they think the answer would be.

**Questions for OE**

What do you like to do? *(sing in the car, dance, play games, play boccia)*

What is your favorite day of the week? *(Friday)*

What is your favorite color? *(pink)*

Who is your coach? *(Austin)*

What does he teach you about boccia? *(softer boccia balls roll slower, kissing the Jack can help you win)*

**Questions for Austin**

What do you coach? *(boccia)*

Why do you coach boccia? *(I have played for over 20 years and traveled the world competing in the Paralympics.)*

What have you won? *(gold medals)*

How do you get OE's attention? *(gently kicking her wheelchair)*

What do you teach OE? *(different boccia balls feel differently, kissing the Jack means getting the boccia balls closest to the Jack, you can go to the Olympics even if you use a wheelchair)*

Self-awareness competency: examining prejudices and biases, identifying personal, cultural, and linguistic assets

OE Wants It to Be Friday

## *An OE Book Report*

Name_____     Date_____

When I read this book, I felt _____ because _____

_____.

The main characters' names are _____.

The story takes place at _____.

The best part of the story is when _____

_____.

I learned _____

_____ from reading this book.

Self-awareness competency: examining prejudices and biases, identifying personal, cultural, and linguistic assets

Finding My Way SEL Curriculum

## SEL Activities Key

### I Don't Know If I Want a Puppy
#### Family Feelings
Ethan **doesn't know** how he feels.

When Emma first comes to Ethan's home, Emma is **scared**.

When Mom knows that Joe and Jake don't want Emma, Mom is **sad**.

When Ethan plays with Emma, Ethan is **happy**.

#### Finding My Purpose
*Colored bones:*
 Ethan likes to give Emma kisses.
 Ethan likes to go outside with Emma.
 Ethan likes to roll around with Emma.
 Ethan likes to be with Emma.

Ethan's purpose is to make his mom worry about Emma. NO

Ethan's purpose is to take care of Emma so his mom won't worry about Emma. YES

### Kaitlyn Wants to See Ducks
#### What Are My Feelings?
Kaitlyn sees 7 animals.

#### It's Hard to Wait
*Things Kaitlyn did while she was waiting:*
 watched water falling
 looked at other animals
 had a ride on Dad's back

### Marco and I Want to Play Ball
#### Playing Fair

When it's time to pick up balls, Marco and Isiah pick them up.
When the ball gets stuck in a tree, Isiah and Marco get it out together.
Marco and Isiah take turns batting the ball.
Isiah and Marco show each other when they catch or drop a ball.

### I Want to Be Like Poppin' Joe
#### Getting Things in Order
Poppin' Joe's job:
 2
 6
 1
 3
 5
 4

Playing ball: (order will differ based on student's home situation)
 5
 6
 4
 3
 1
 2

### Waylen Wants to Jam
#### Learning to Play the Drum
Sal tells us to **hold in** our sticks.
Sal tells us to place our sticks like a slice of **pizza**.
Sal shows us a stick **trick**.
Sal teaches us how to play a **song**.
Sal shows us a **silly** pose.
Sal tells us we need to **listen** when playing on the **drumline**.

# Finding My Way SEL Student Survey

Name_____    Date_____

**Circle the emoji that best fits you.**

|  | Don't know what to do! | Get nervous. Do nothing. | Smile | Talk |
|---|---|---|---|---|
| What do I do when I meet someone in a wheelchair? | 😲 | 😐 | 🙂 | 😃 |
| What do I do when I meet someone who looks different because of a disability? | 😲 | 😐 | 🙂 | 😃 |
| What do I do when I want to play with someone with a disability? | 😲 | 😐 | 🙂 | 😃 |
| What do I do when I want to talk to someone I know with a disability? | 😲 | 😐 | 🙂 | 😃 |
| How do I feel about being an inclusive friend? | 😲 | 😐 | 🙂 | 😃 |

# Data Collection for Finding My Way SEL curriculum

Organization: _____ Prepared by:_____

Number of participants: _____ Pre-survey date: _____ Post-survey date: _____

**Description**: Each survey contains the following questions with responses selected from an Emoji Likert type scale.

1. What do I do when I meet someone in a wheelchair?
2. What do I do when I meet someone who looks different because of a disability?
3. What do I do when I want to play with someone with a disability?
4. What do I do when I want to talk to someone I know with a disability?
5. How do I feel about being an inclusive friend?

**Scoring**: Each Emoji has an assigned value. Total the number of responses for each Emoji.
*Don't Know what to do! = 1*
*Get nervous. Do nothing = 2*
*Smile = 3*
*Talk = 4*

Multiply the number of participants X 5 questions to identify the total number of responses. _____
Divide the number of responses per Emoji by the total to get percentage scores.

Pre-survey:

- _____% of the responses were *'Don't know what to do!'*
- _____% of the responses were *'Get nervous. Do nothing'*
- _____% of the responses were *'Smile'*
- _____% of the responses were *'Talk'*

Post-survey:

- _____% of the responses were *'Don't know what to do!'*
- _____% of the responses were *'Get nervous. Do nothing'*
- _____% of the responses were *'Smile'*
- _____% of the responses were *'Talk'*

**Summary**: Compare the pre- and post-survey results to provide a general overview of change in participants' attitudes. For additional information you can score each question to identify more specifically where attitude changes occurred. Also, consider including anecdotal data and staff observations during the program.

# *Finding My Way Certificate*

Social and Emotional Learning

## Self-Awareness Award

**For understanding how I feel!**

**Awarded to**

_____

_____
*Signature and Date*

www.ingramcontent.com/pod-product-compliance
Lightning Source LLC
Chambersburg PA
CBHW051400110526
44592CB00023B/2904